ISBN 978-0-428-12079-5
PIBN 11248139

What Farm Families Spend for Medical Care

U. S. DEPARTMENT OF AGRICULTURE
Miscellaneous Publication No. 561

This report has been prepared in the Family Economics Division under the direction of Helen R. Jeter. The data were collected as part of a study of Family Spending and Saving in Wartime by the Bureau of Human Nutrition and Home Economics of the United States Department of Agriculture, in cooperation with the Bureau of Labor Statistics of the United States Department of Labor. The figures cover the year 1941 and were collected early in 1942. Further details from this study of expenditures for medical care will be found in Rural Family Spending and Saving in Wartime, United States Department of Agriculture Miscellaneous Publication 520; a forthcoming publication of the United States Bureau of Labor Statistics, Income, Spending and Saving of American Families; and in Medical Care and Costs in Relation to Family Income, A Statistical Source Book, Social Security Board, Bureau of Research and Statistics Bureau Memorandum 51.

HAZEL K. STIEBELING, Chief
Bureau of Human Nutrition and
Home Economics

INTRODUCTION

w possessions more important to man than
cannot be sure that every citizen has an
ity to share in the services that medical
provide toward maintaining health. Medi-
noney and it is unequally distributed. Par-
true in rural areas. Families are widely
me in general is low. Hospitals and scien-
necessary to the practice of modern medi-
g in some areas, inadequate in others.

s aggravated the situation. In many rural
ber of physicians had been slowly declining
r. The needs of the armed forces took many

t as the decline in numbers, however, has
line in efficiency. Rural physicians are be-
l men of the profession. Their training was in
f the past. The isolation of rural practice
ically impossible for them to keep abreast of
ine.

duates of the medical schools, even those from
re not settling in rural areas. They prefer to
they can earn an adequate living, consult
ns, and have access to hospitals and other
ssary to continued advancement in their pro-
younger physicians now in the armed forces
to the rural areas where they practiced, but
movement to the cities.

le are searching for solutions to these prob-
new methods of providing medical care for
are tried out, collection of more data to guide
s goes on. This publication is written to assist
n of postwar problems. Its purpose is to con-
nformation needed for a successful solution to
f making available to every family the full
knowledge and resources of the medical pro-
ostacle to such solution is cost.

This discussion is limited to medical expenses met direc
by families. In most instances, it is still the family that be
the major burden of providing medical care in time of
ness, although the community assists through taxation a
endowment in providing special equipment and servic
The expenditures shown here are the actual practice
families. They are not a guide to what must be spent
provide adequate care. They represent only money pc
out or debts incurred and give no indication of the qual
of medical care received.

The report is divided into three parts. Part 1 gives inf
mation about the medical care expenses of farm famili
at various income levels. Part 2 discusses the differen
between average expenses for large groups of famili
and what happens to the family pocketbook when illn
strikes a particular family. Part 3 contrasts rural and urb
expenditures for medical care.

Expenditures for medical care are grouped in this rep
in the following classifications: Services of physicia
specialists, and surgeons, referred to as physicians' ca
dental care; eye care, including refractions and glass
hospital care; medicines and drugs; and all other. Includ
in "all other" are care by other practitioners, clinic ca
X-ray examination or treatment, nursing care, medical a
pliances and supplies, and prepayment for medical ca

Farm families are defined as those operating far
farm laborers are not included in the farm group. Urb
families are those in incorporated places of 2,500 po
lation or more. Rural nonfarm families, for brevity call
village families, are those in towns of less than 2,500 po
lation, in unincorporated places, and in the open coun
but not operating farms. Income is money income only, c
does not include the value of home-produced food c
fuel, or the rental value of owned homes.

The data are from a sample of all families in the Uni
States, representative of economic level, distribution
rural and urban population, type of farming or ot
occupation.

do patterns in their spending for medical care come into view. Then some differences and some similarities in their medical expenses can be traced.

As farm families' incomes increase, they spend more money on medical care, but this money is a smaller proportion of their incomes. Since in higher income groups families spend more money for other living expenses also, the relationship between the amount spent for medical care and the amount spent for other living expenses remains about the same.

Almost all farm families buy some type of medical care, but the proportion of families buying care is higher among those families whose incomes are higher. Low-income families are faced with the necessity of choosing which type of care they will buy more frequently than families with higher incomes. They report expenditures for physician or dentist when higher income families report expenditures for both physician and dentist. Consequently, the proportion of families buying each type of care increases more rapidly than the proportion buying any care at all.

Since relatively more families at high-income levels buy medical care and since they buy more types of care than low-income families, it is not surprising to find that their expenditures for medical care are higher than those of low-income families. They also spend larger amounts on most of the items of care they buy.

Because of these differences among income groups in the amounts spent for each type of medical care and the variety of care purchased, the relative importance of the medication. Families with higher incomes spend more for the physician and for medicines and drugs, but their use of some of the other types of medical care increases at a greater rate. Because of their increased expenditure for hospitalization, nursing, and miscellaneous care, the proportion of their medical care dollar going for physicians' care is slightly less, and the proportion going for medicines and drugs is much less than the proportions of the medical care dollar of low-income families for these same types of care.

All these facts might be interpreted to mean that ill health rises as income increases. This is not the case. Studies of the incidence of illness show that there is more illness among low-income families than among those with high incomes. The latter, however, can afford to buy more preventive care and more treatment for the illnesses they do incur. The pressure of other demands on a limited income keeps many farm families from arranging for the medical care they need.

Sufficient income to purchase medical care, however, will not in itself assure the family good care. There must be an opportunity to obtain good care and the realization that it is advantageous. These conditions do not always exist among farm families. The relatively large proportion of higher income farm families reporting no expenditure for dental care during the year covered by this study, for example, indicates that even with money to spend some farm families do not spend it on medical care.

These facts are shown graphically in the following pages.

FARM FAMILIES DEVOTE A UNIFORM SHARE OF THEIR LIVING EXPENSES AT DIFFERENT INCOME LEVELS TO MEDICAL CARE

If large numbers of families are grouped by size of income, the average expenditure for medical care is about the same proportion of the average living cost for each group.

THE SHARE MEDICAL CARE TAKES OF LIVING EXPENSES AMONG FAMILIES

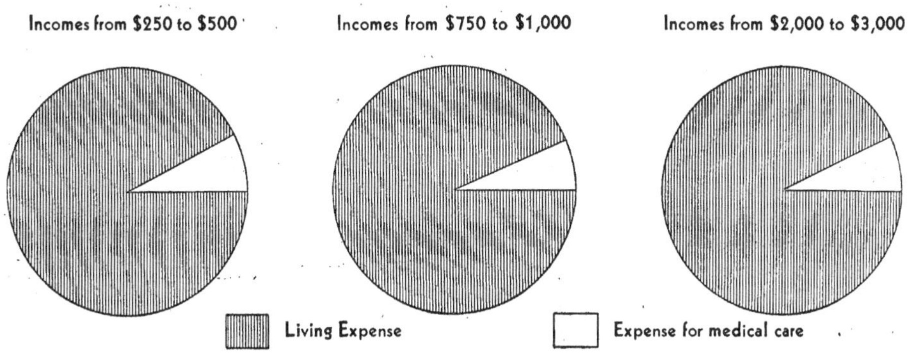

FARM FAMILIES SPEND A DECREASING SHARE OF THEIR TOTAL INCOME ON MEDICAL CARE AS THEIR INCOMES INCREASE

Among low-income families almost the whole income, sometimes more than the year's income, must be spent for family living. As income increases, families use a smaller proportion of it for living expenses and are able to save more. Consequently, expenditures for medical care take a larger share of a small than of a large income.

THE SHARE MEDICAL CARE TAKES OF INCOME AMONG FAMILIES

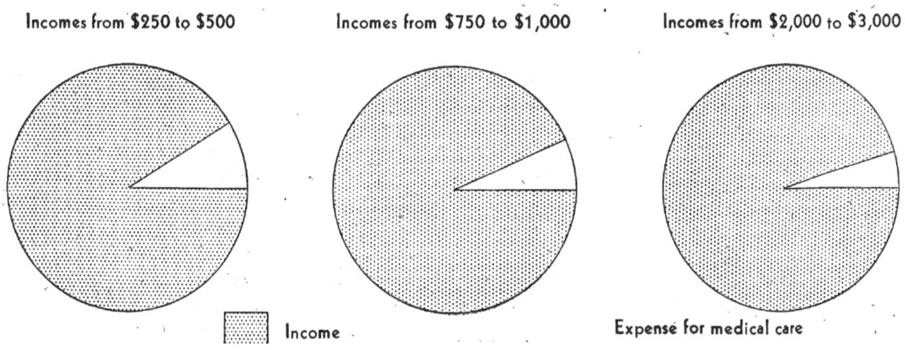

THEIR INCOMES INCREASE, A LARGER PROPORTION OF FARM FAMILIES BUY MEDICAL CARE

nost all families spend something for medical in the course of a year, but the percentage of ies spending for certain types of care varies with ie. Families with low income are less likely to buy some types of care than families in better circumstances. This is particularly true of dental care and hospital care.

PERCENTAGE OF FAMILIES BUYING THESE TYPES OF CARE

INCOMES FROM $250 TO $500

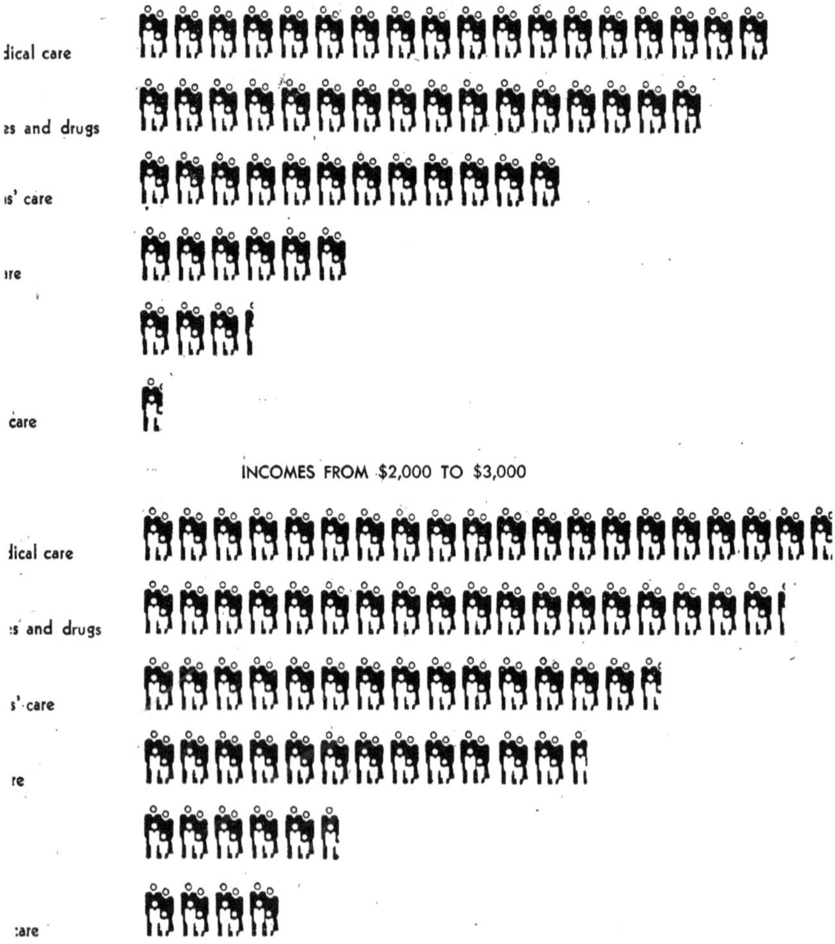

FARM FAMILIES SPEND MORE MONEY FOR MEDICA
AS THEIR INCOMES INCREASE

Partly because a larger proportion of families buy medical care in high-income groups than in low, and partly because certain families in the high-income groups spend more, the average expenditure for medical care rises with income. Families with incomes from $2,000 to $3,000 spend more for physicians' care alone than fam from $250 to $500 spend for all. all care they spend more than three this lower income group.

AVERAGE MEDICAL EXPENSES OF FAMILIES FOR THESE TYPES

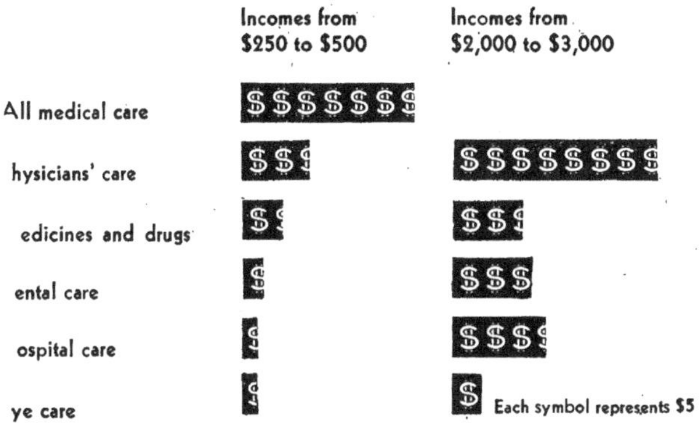

ARM FAMILIES WITH HIGHER INCOMES BUY MORE TYI

Few farm families receive medical care without cost and the free care received by these few is largely limited to hospital care and physicians' care. Free care is not, however, confined to the lowest income groups. Relatively more families with incomes from $750 to $1,000—the middle-income group among farm families—received free care than in any other income group. "Free care" includes "charity work" by physicians, care received without cost from philanthropic institutions, Government agencies and employers, care received from relatives and friends, and "professional courtesy" extended to the families of other professional persons.

PERCENTAGE OF FAMILIES RECEIVING FREE MEDICAL CARE

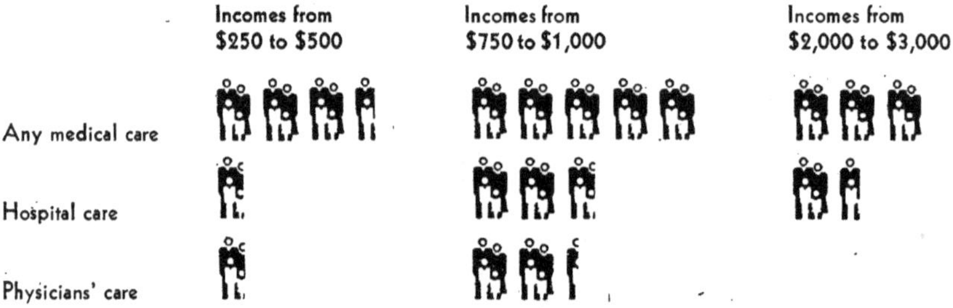

Each symbol represents 2 percent of all families in the income class

HOW FARM FAMILIES SPEND THEIR MEDICAL DOLLAR

Although the amount spent for each type of medical care increases with income in almost all cases, the proportion of the total medical expense used for certain items decreases. Among those items for which a decreasing proportion is spent as income increases are physicians' care, medicines and drugs, and eye care. Hospital care and "all other" take an increasing share. The proportion spent for dental care remains about the same at various levels of income.

Families with incomes from $250 to $500 spend this way

Families with incomes from $2,000 to $3,000 spend this way

which the medical expenses of a certain family may fall is very wide. Moreover, it is impossible to predict the amount of illness and the consequent expense that any particular family will have in any given year.

Average yearly expenditures for medical care have significance for the individual family only when they are considered in relation to the amount it may expect to have to spend in the course of its lifetime; it has little significance for the family's annual budget. In a given year very few families will spend an amount equivalent to the average expenditures of a group for medical care. For most families in any income group the year's expenditures will be far below the average. For a few it will be well above. There is no tendency for the expenditures of individual families to cluster around the average as is the case with most other major expenditures for family living.

Medical expenses may be separated into two kinds. The first, which may be termed "normal" expenditures, includes treatment of the ordinary run of minor illnesses or chronic conditions and some preventive care. A very large proportion of the families in any income group will incur expenses of this kind only. They will be the families with small expenditures. A few families in any income group, however, will suffer serious illnesses or accidents—"catastrophic" illnesses, so-called because of their unpredictable and overwhelming nature. These are the families whose expenditures will be many times the normal amount and may consume a large part of the year's total income.

While not all hospitalized illnesses are catastrophic, and conversely, not all catastrophic illnesses are hospitalized, the group of families that incurred expenses for hospital care during the course of the year may be considered representative of families suffering catastrophic illnesses. The total expenditures for medical care in families that had hospital expenses were about triple the expenditures of care. No one type of service is responsible for the high cost of catastrophic illness.

Among families with high medical expenses, expenditures for physicians, dentists, and refractions and eyeglasses are more important than with families whose medical expenses are low. The latter spend more than half their medical dollar for medicines and drugs. Since the study on which these charts are based was a study of money expenditures, it provides no data concerning the amount of free medical care obtained by families or the circumstances under which it was received. Other studies have shown, however, that it is for catastrophic illness that most free care is given. Many families able to meet their normal medical expenditures are unable to bear the cost of catastrophic illness.

Because the family has so little control over the amount it may be called upon to spend for medical care, the effects of these expenditures on its financial management are significant. When a family is faced with a medical bill, it may meet it out of current income, it may draw on previous savings, or it may go into debt. In the long run the family may adjust other expenditures to balance the medical bill or it may reduce its current and accrued savings. The medical bills of that part of the group with heavy medical expenses are frequently high enough to make total expenditures for family living greater than the year's total income and to preclude any saving during the year.

To illustrate the possible variations in expenditures among families with approximately the same income, the expenditures of farm families in the median-income group are analyzed in the following pages. These families had incomes from $750 to $1,000. The general statements made about this group will hold true for other income groups also, although the exact figures will differ.

THE FAMILIES THAT INCUR THE EXPENSE PAY THE BILLS

Average costs for all families are useful when considering the costs of medical care for the entire population. They are meaningless, however, when the actual costs of families that pay the bills are under consideration. Not all families have expenditures for any medical care or for each type of care. When families without expense are eliminated, the average of the bills to be met by those families that actually incurred the expense becomes larger. If a certain type of expense, such as for medicines, is incurred by a large proportion of families, the difference between the average cost to all families and the average cost to families paying the bills is small; if the expense is incurred by a few families only, such as that for hospital care, the difference in the averages may be very great.

AVERAGE MEDICAL EXPENSES OF MIDDLE-INCOME FARM FAMILIES

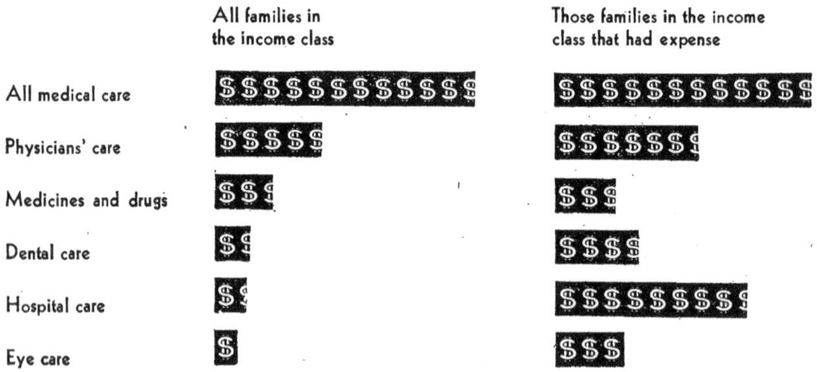

Each symbol represents $5

WHEN SOMEONE GOES TO THE HOSPITAL, EXPENSE FOR MEDICAL CARE SHOOTS UP

In general, families that have hospital bills are among those who spend most for medical care. Among farm families with incomes from $750 to $1,000, they spend over three times as much as families that have no hospital bills. The hospital bill is only part of the total cost of illness that requires hospital care. Physicians' bills increase, particularly if surgery is involved. There may be a nurse's bill or bills for X-rays and laboratory services.

AMOUNT SPENT FOR ALL MEDICAL CARE BY MIDDLE-INCOME FARM FAMILIES

Each symbol represents $5

AL EXPENSES OF MANY FAMILIES ARE NOT BURDENSOME

for medical care that must be met in a vary widely. Some families spend nothing, ch as $500. In any one year the expendi- most two-thirds of the families are well below the average of the group. The small bills of many families are in sharp contrast to the very large bills of a few.

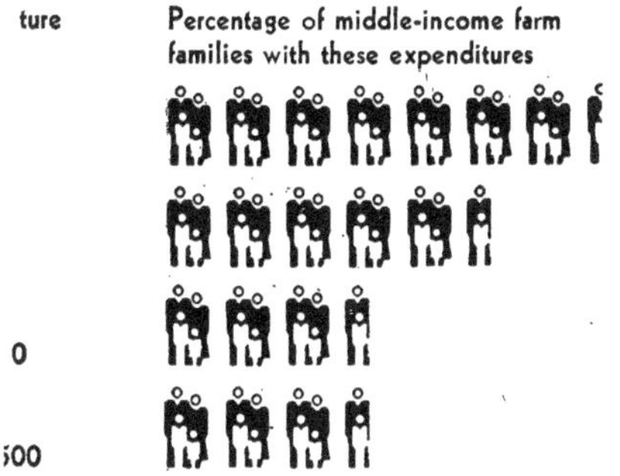

Each symbol represents 5 percent of families

OMPOSITION OF MEDICAL BILL VARIES WITH ITS SIZE

he total expenditure for medical care is licines and drugs account for more than ınd physicians' care for slightly more than a ıs might be expected, the third of the fami- ad the least expense for medical care re- expenditures whatever for hospital care. third of the families with the highest medi- xpenses, the largest share—somewhat less than half of the total—was used for physicians' services. Hospitalization took an eighth. The proportions used for eye care and dental care each were larger than among families with low expenditures. Medicines and drugs, on the other hand, although they cost about five times as much for families with high expenditures, consume only a third as much of the total bill as among low-expenditure families.

RIBUTION OF MEDICAL DOLLAR OF MIDDLE-INCOME FARM FAMILIES

Among the third of the families spending least for medical care

Among the third of the families spending most for medical care

They carried this part of the total medical care expense

Each symbol represents 5 percent of the total

YOU CAN'T PREDICT THE SLICE MEDICAL CARE WILL TAKE

If farm families with incomes from $750 to $1,000 are divided into three groups according to the amount spent for medical care, the cost to the third spending least is negligible—about 1 percent of total income. The cost to the middle third, about 4 percent of income, can be met without strain also. But an expenditure of 15 percent of total income for medical care, the amount required of the third with highest expenditures, may well prove burdensome.

PROPORTION OF INCOME USED FOR MEDICAL EXPENSES BY MIDDLE-INCOME FARM FAMILIES

The third of the families spending least for medical care

The middle third as to medical care expenses

The third of the families spending most for medical care

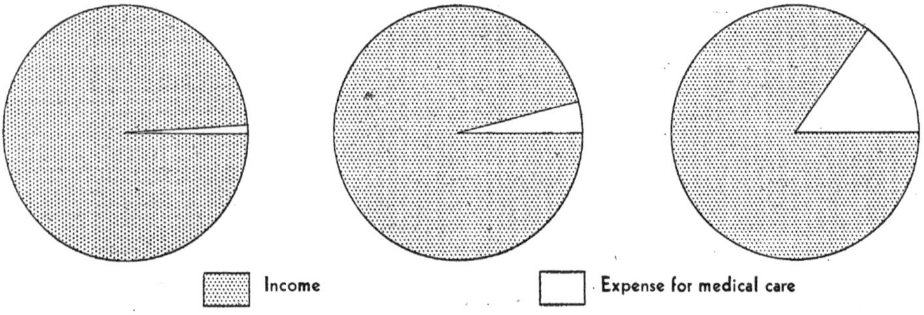

VER FAMILIES CAN SAVE WHEN MEDICAL EXPENSES ARE HIGH

edical care is not the only item that may throw amily budget out of balance, but it is a frequent e. Among farm families with incomes from $750 ,000 the proportion of families with high expense for medical care whose living expenses exceed their income is almost twice the proportion of those with low expense for medical care.

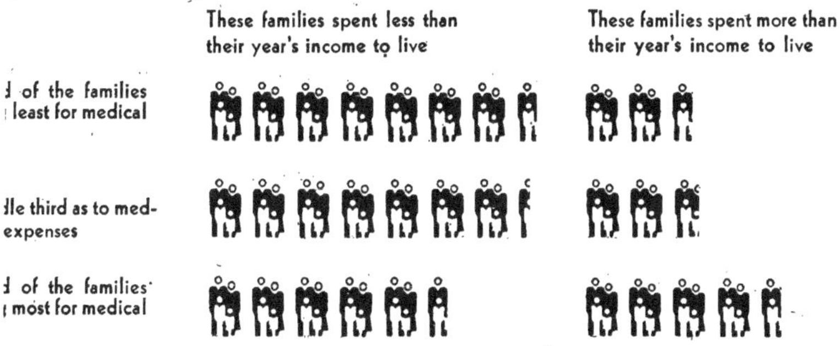

Each symbol represents 10 percent of middle-income farm families

AMILIES CAN SAVE LESS WHEN MEDICAL EXPENSES ARE HIGH

There are differences as well as similarities in the spending patterns of farm and urban families where medical care is concerned. Underlying the differences in the amounts spent for medical care by these families is the fundamental difference in money income between the two groups. Farm families spend slightly more for medical care than urban families with the same money incomes. This fact, however, is of no actual significance for the group as a whole, since most farm families spend less for medical care than most urban families because their incomes are lower. In 1941 the median net cash income of farm families was less than half that of urban families. Comparisons are made in this section between median-income farm families and median-income urban families since they represent average conditions for the two groups.

Middle-income farm families spend less for medical c than middle-income urban families. Since farm families larger than urban families, this disparity is even grea when the figures are translated from expenditures family to expenditures per person.

In cities, as on farms, almost all families buy some type medical care. Among median-income families, the prop tion of families spending for physicians' care is the sa on farms, in villages, and in cities and towns. The perce age buying hospital care, dental care, and eye care, ho ever, is greater among urban than among rural famil On the other hand, a larger share of the medical expen tures of middle-income farm families than of urban fami goes for physicians' care, medicines and drugs, and e care, while a smaller share goes to dental and hosp care.

HOW MIDDLE-INCOME FAMILIES SPEND THEIR MEDICAL DOLLAR

Middle-income farm families spend a larger part of their medical care dollar than middle-income families in towns and cities for physicians' care, medicines and drugs, and eye care. They spend a smaller part for dental and hospital care, and for all other items.

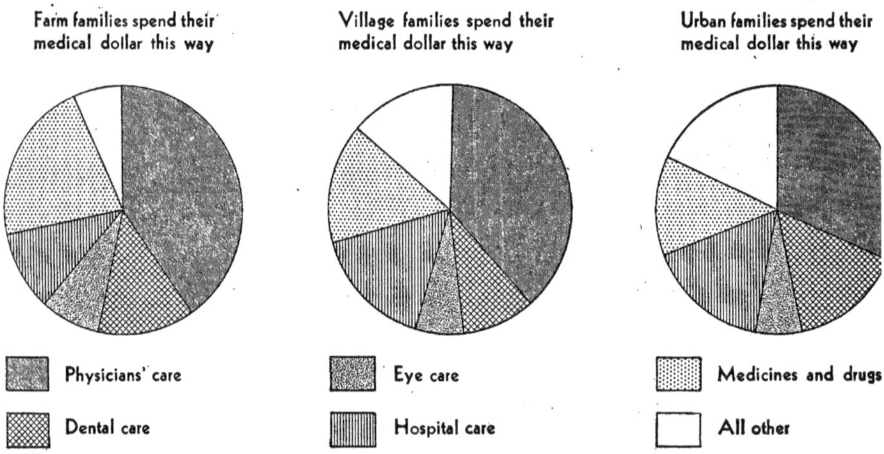

M FAMILIES SPEND LESS THAN URBAN FAMILIES FOR THE MEDICAL CARE OF EACH MEMBER

farm families spend somewhat more for than urban families with similar incomes, ture per person is smaller. Farm families are larger than urban families; the money they spend must cover the care of more people.

FAMILIES SPEND THESE AMOUNTS PER PERSON

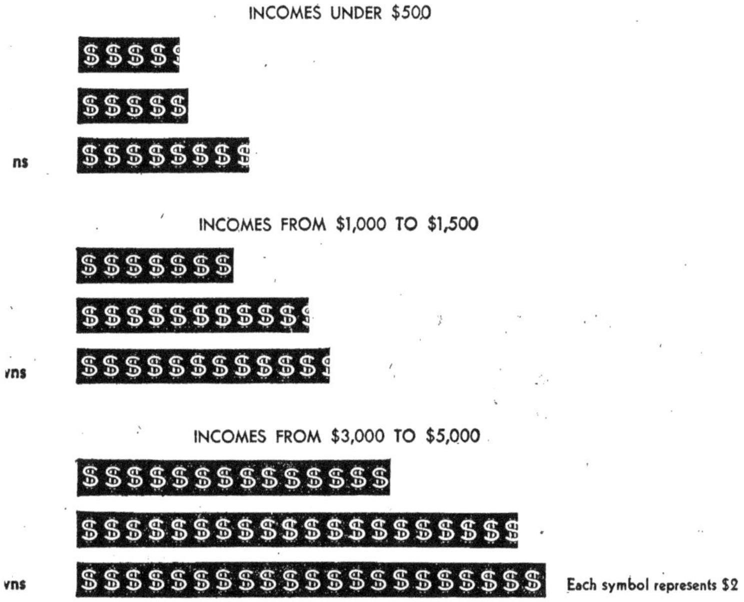

T MIDDLE-INCOME FAMILIES SPEND FOR MEDICAL CARE

me is lower than urban; farm families are ddle-income farm families, with incomes to $1,000, spent two-thirds as much for medical care as middle-income city families with incomes from $1,500 to $2,000. They spent a little more than half as much per member.

MIDDLE-INCOME FAMILIES BUY THESE AMOUNTS OF CARE

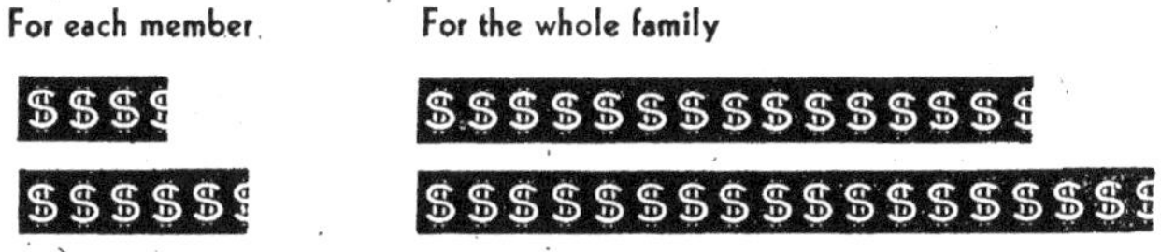

for medical care by the urban families is greater than that spent by farm or village families. More than half

incomes u
have inco

ON FARMS

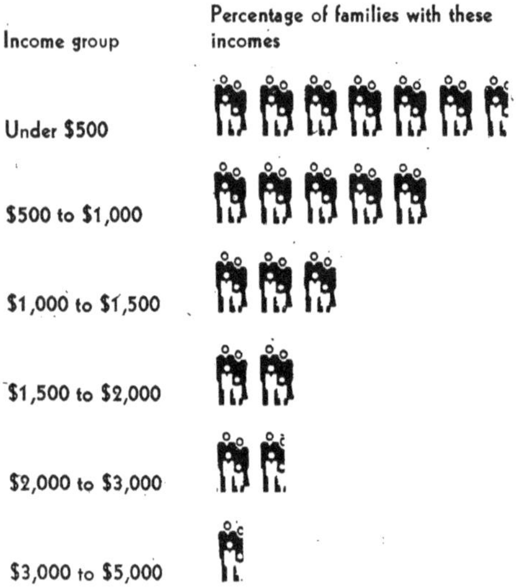

Each symbol represents 5 percent of all families in each type of community

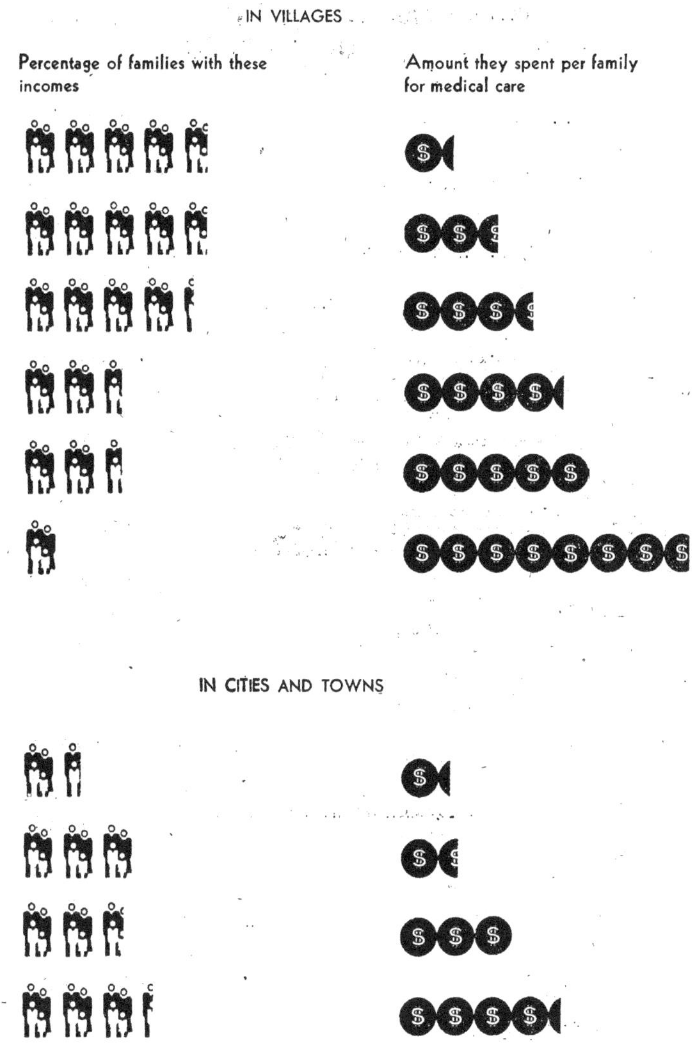
IN VILLAGES
Percentage of families with these incomes
Amount they spent per family for medical care
IN CITIES AND TOWNS

THESE FAMILIES BOUGHT THESE TYPES OF CARE

ON FARMS

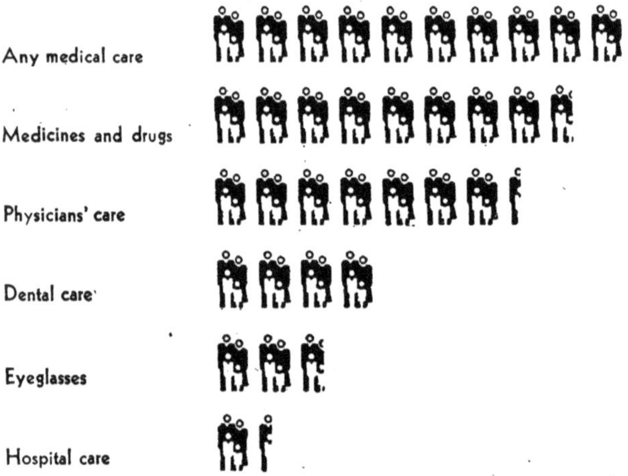

Each symbol represents 10 percent of the families in the income group

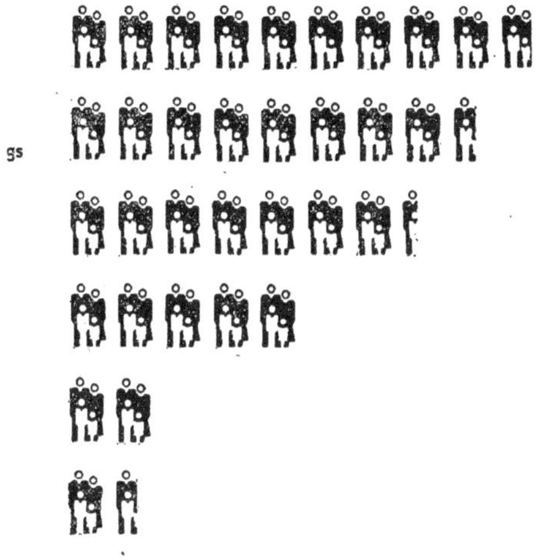

IN CITIES AND TOWNS

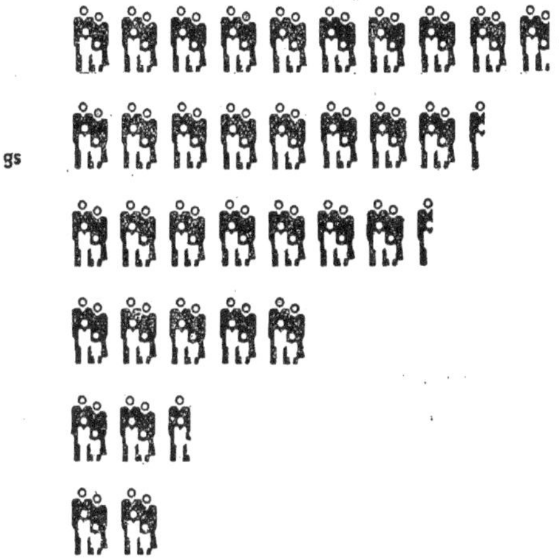

Each symbol represents 10 percent of the families in the income group

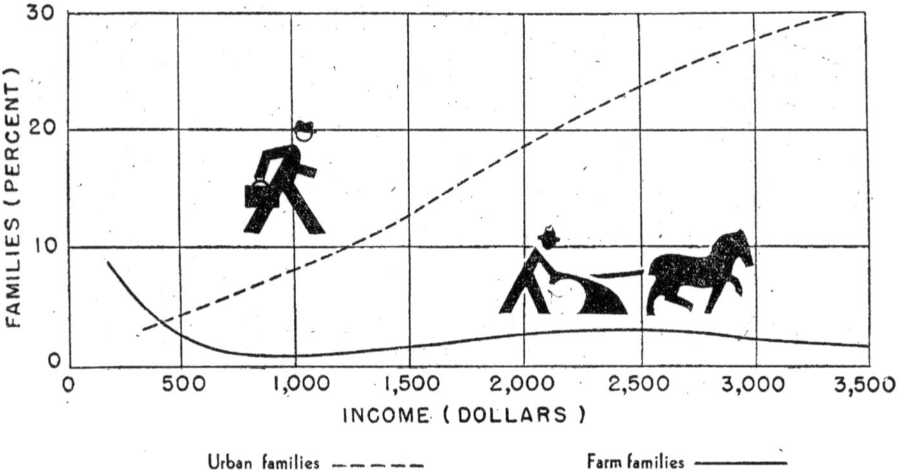

Prepared by

BUREAU OF HUMAN NUTRITION AND HOME ECONOMICS

Agricultural Research Administration

United States Department of Agriculture

Washington, D. C.

April 1945

☆ U. S. GOVERNMENT PRINTING OFFICE : 1945—634900

CPSIA information can be obtained
at www.ICGtesting.com
Printed in the USA
LVHW080808051218
599325LV00003B/274/P